Clay: the potter's wheel

Clay: the potter's wheel

Maurice Sapiro

Photographs by
Erwin Sapiro
and the Author

Davis Publications, Inc.
Worcester, Massachusetts

Acknowledgements

William Hunt, Managing Editor, *Ceramics Monthly,* for initiating the compulsive desire to write; **Morton Handler,** former Managing Editor, *Arts and Activities,* for his enthusiastic encouragement in the early days (when it was most needed); **George Horn,** Editor, *School Arts,* for acting as consultant for this book; **Susan Trewartha,** Editor, Davis Publications, for her valuable suggestions, and her compatible editorial manner; *School Arts,* and *Arts and Activities,* for reprint permission on the items that first appeared as magazine articles; and to those brilliant Chinese potters of over four thousand years ago who started it all;

I offer my thanks.

Maurice Sapiro
February 1978

Printed in the United States of America
Library of Congress Catalog Card Number: 77-084480
ISBN: 0-87192-095-6

Consulting Editors: George F. Horn and Sarita R. Rainey

10 9 8 7 6 5

Contents

Foreword

Learning to throw on the potter's wheel, acquiring the skills and techniques necessary to transform a rotating mass of clay into a functional, aesthetic form, is a challenging, sometimes frustrating, often rewarding venture. In an effort to make the learning and teaching process meaningful and productive, this book presents lessons based on the concept of throwing geometric shapes. By mastering a series of basic shapes, one can learn to create both simple and complex forms on the potter's wheel. Each chapter presents examples of final products that evolve from these basic shapes. As these objects vary in size and difficulty, personal growth can be determined by one's ability, interest, and a desire for individual expression. Unique items have also been included to stimulate the student to learn and create. These projects are intended as merely stepping-stones. The manual manipulations learned in this book will allow the potter to pursue other personal goals on the wheel.

The objects presented and demonstrated reflect my personal preference for ceramic products that are functional, innovative, and based solidly on tradition. My choices are not meant to narrow the student's interests, attempts, and personal pursuits. It is right for the individual with two hands on the wheel, to steer a personal course.

Notably absent in books on ceramics is a potter's wheel learning-teaching guide, progressively arranged, that allows a variety of final products to evolve at each developmental stage. This book responds to this need. The exercises offer a development of skills in a progressive order: the cylinder leading to the oval, the oval to the bowl. The advanced techniques of double-wall cylinder throwing, and creating sculpture from thrown forms, complete the learning process. Each subsequent chapter uses previously learned skills, introduces new techniques, and extends the student potter's technical vocabulary.

Proficiency is accompanied by confidence. The throwing of a pot soon becomes a series of controlled reflexes, and hands function without premeditation. Hesitant efforts are replaced with sure, deft movements. A rhythm is established, and the individual processes of centering, opening, and drawing up, all proceed from one to the other in a continuous flow. Success initiates success. A form quickly arrived at maintains an innate strength, allowing far greater flexibility in the final design, while overworked clay is unresponsive.

To all who share my concern with the task of imparting form, meaning, and that elusive quality of timeless beauty to a mass of cohesive mud, using their hands, mind, eye, and a spinning disc, I dedicate this book.

For Sally, John, and Sarah

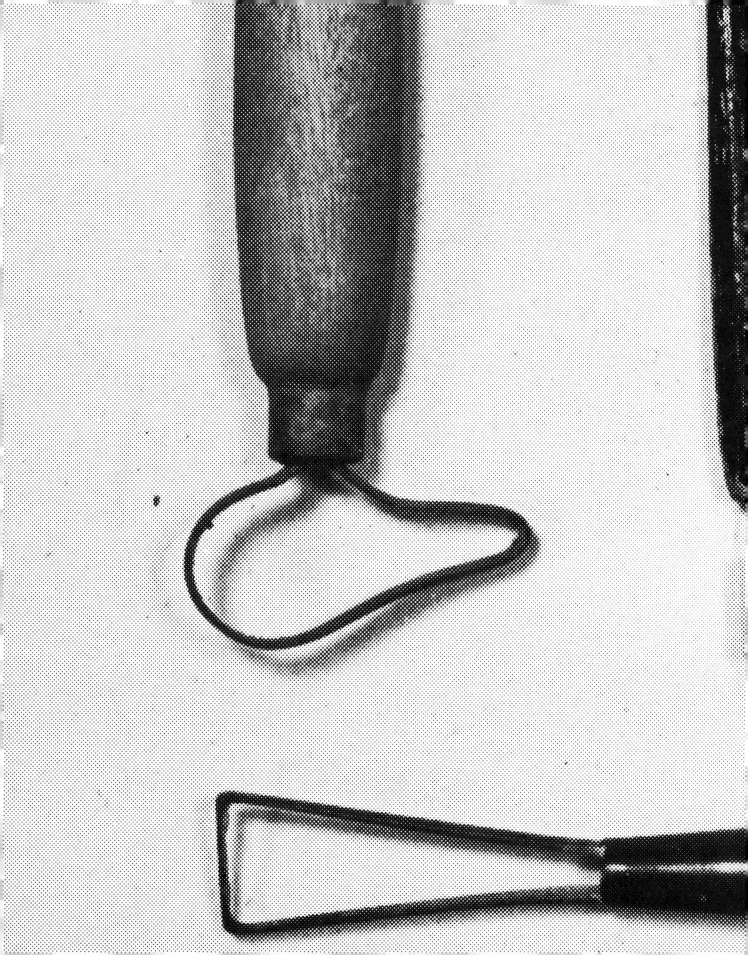

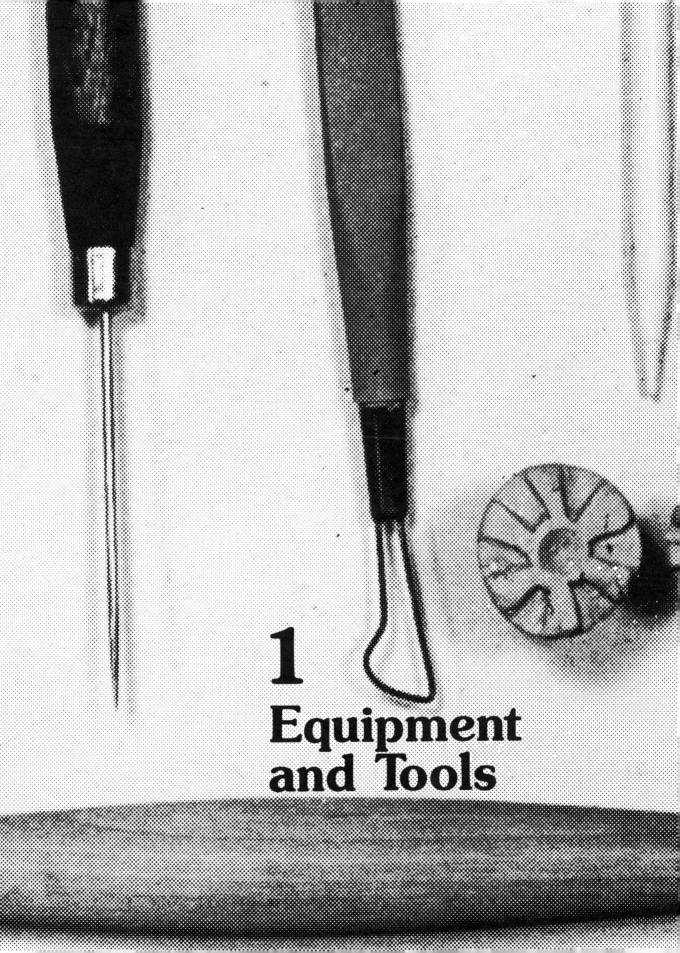

1
Equipment and Tools

Equipment and Tools

A revolving disc, a pair of hands, and clay complete the list of basic material requirements necessary for wheel throwing. Additional equipment will serve only as supplements to these basics.

The Wheel

Ceramic supply houses offer a wide variety of potter's wheels. Mechanically or electronically controlled motor driven wheels are available in either two-speed or variable speed models. Kick wheels with or without motor assistance are manufactured in an endless array of designs.

Some manufacturers offer the option of wheel rotation in either direction. Throughout this book, the wheel rotation is in a counterclockwise direction, the standard of the Western world; and all instruction is based on this standard.

A decision as to what wheel is best is open to many considerations, and can be solved by throwing attempts on the various types. If this experimentation is not possible, a motor driven, variable speed wheel is recommended, as it allows full concentration on clay manipulation; no physical effort is needed to propel the wheel. Excellent models are available with either method of speed regulation.

Clay

Clay, the resultant end product of the effects of time and environmental forces upon rock containing feldspar, will rarely be found in its natural state possessing the qualities necessary for wheel throwing. Different clays will vary as to firing temperature, color, and plasticity. The cohesiveness that allows the manipulations and formations that take place on the rotating wheel head is best arrived at by a combination of clays and minerals, the resulting mix called the "clay body."

Stoneware clays possess a natural plasticity. A cone 6 firing range will not only allow a throwable clay body, but the firing range is still low enough to represent an energy saving firing cycle, while remaining within the range of a high-fire electric kiln.

If a plastic clay body is not readily available, a specially made clay body using the following formula may be ordered from a ceramic supply house offering a custom blending service:

Formula for a plastic stoneware clay cone 6 to 10
Jordan Stoneware Clay...................... 60 parts
Ball Clay, Ky. Special........................20 parts
Flint, 200 mesh............................... 10 parts
Feldspar, Custer............................. 10 parts
Add: Iron Oxide, Black (for color).......1%
           Grog, 40—80 mesh..................4%

Tools

Any tool to be used in throwing should be thought of as a supplement to the fingers. Only when the task cannot be accomplished by the fingers, should a tool be utilized.

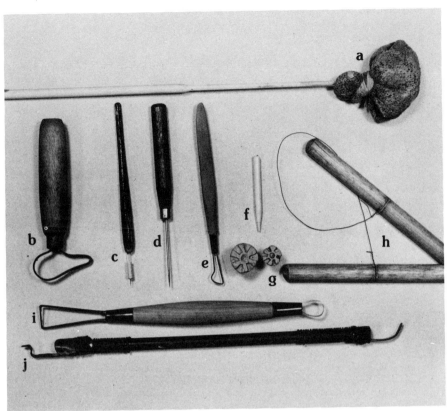

A selection of the most useful potter's tools. Their use should be confined to serving only as supplementary aids to the hands.

a. Sponge stick
b. Wire cutter
c. Needle tool, taped for thickness checking
d. Needle tool
e. Wire cutter
f. Pointed plastic rod
g. Bisqued clay stamps
h. Cut-off wire
i. Wire cutter
j. Homemade trimmer
k. Wood modeling tools
l. Calipers
m. Rubber kidney
n. Steel kidney
o. Wood palette
p. Elephant ear sponge

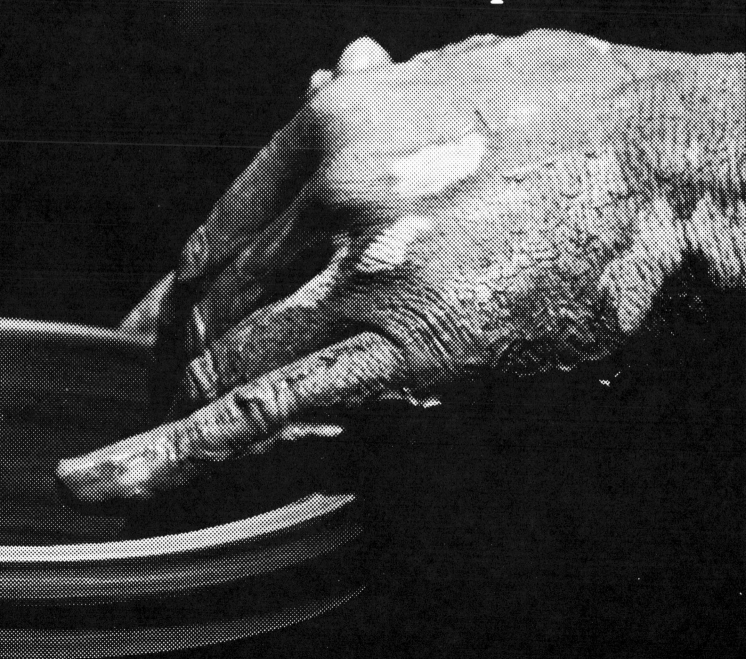

2
Teaching
Basic Throwing
Techniques

Teaching Basic Throwing Techniques

For the beginner, the actual feeling of a rotating ball of clay forming within the hands proves to be a very meaningful learning experience. Four hands are better than two—especially for teaching or learning the basic techniques of throwing on a potter's wheel.

In this setup, student and teacher sit at opposite sides of the wheel, both having comfortable access to the wheel head. During the entire first effort, the student should be along ''just for the ride''—hands in contact with the clay, but exerting no pressure. Basic hand positions are formed by imitation. As the clay passes through each stage in the forming process, the student actually experiences the manipulations necessary to shape the clay.

This throwing lesson proceeds in three stages.

I. Centering

A four pound ball of clay will provide enough room for four hands. The clay should be a plastic throwing body, and thoroughly wedged—that is, blended. A clay with a soft, wet consistency will facilitate the learning of the centering process, as it is more manageable and less resistant than the stiffer clay body normally used on the wheel.

Form the clay into a ball and place it in the center of the wheel head. Water is applied as lubrication, and the wheel is rotated at a fast speed. First the teacher, then the student place their hands on the clay, and the centering process begins. The transition from an off-centered mass of clay, bumping the hands, to a smoothly rotating form, with no noticeable lateral movement demonstrates quickly the feel of a correctly centered ball of clay.

II. Opening

The teacher opens the ball of clay, leaving a bottom thickness of one-quarter inch. The bottom is leveled and widened. A wide opening

Throughout this photo sequence, the student's hands are on the left, the teacher's hands on the right.
Centering—The student, hands in contact with the clay, experiences the tactile sensations of the centering process.

Opening—Again the student manually experiences the movement of the clay.

Widening of the opening not only establishes the cylinder floor, but readies the lower portion of the cylinder wall for subsequent drawing up.

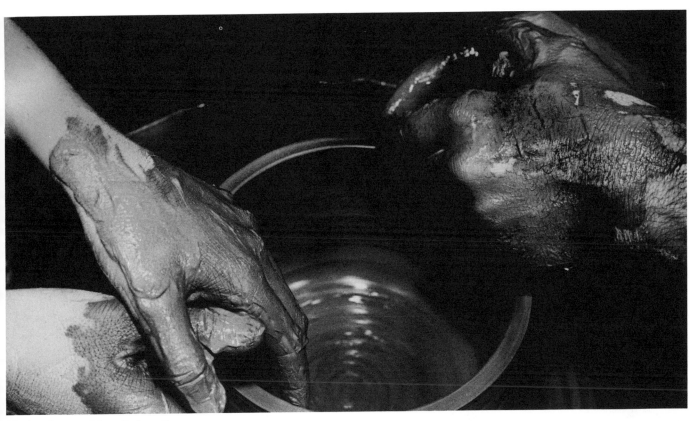

The first draw up of the cylinder wall.

is needed to allow both the teacher's and the student's left hand inside the cylinder. With each movement, the student's hands reflect the position and stance of the teacher's hands.

III. Drawing up the walls

During the drawing up process, one should observe which parts of the fingers come into contact with the walls. It should be emphasized that both hands function as one unit, locked together at the thumbs. Each pull should result in a taller cylinder with thinner walls.

In each subsequent throwing session, the student takes a more active role, until eventually it is the teacher who is there "just for the ride." As the student progresses, a stiffer clay may be used, and emphasis should be placed on thinning the walls to one-quarter inch from the top to the bottom of the cylinder. When all hand positions are mastered, and confidence is gained, the student will be ready for a solo throw.

The wheel speed is slowed, and the cylinder is drawn up to full height.

3
Six Common Mistakes and How to Overcome Them

Six Common Mistakes and How to Overcome Them

Most potters feel that anyone can learn the skills required to throw on the potter's wheel. Yet, they also agree that many hours, and often years, of practicing are needed to acquire these skills. Certain mistakes seem to occur with regularity. Avoiding the common pitfalls will shorten the learning process and bring about success more quickly.

Traditionally, the throwing of cylinders serves as the means of learning the basic techniques. Knowing the techniques needed to throw a tall, thin walled cylinder will equip the potter with the necessary skills to throw any form on the wheel.

The six most recurring mistakes made by the beginning potter on the wheel are:
1. Throwing with improperly wedged clay.
2. Proceeding with the throwing process before the clay is truly centered.
3. Misjudging bottom thickness.
4. Inability to thin the lower portion of the cylinder wall.
5. Inability to keep the cylinder walls parallel.
6. Over-wetting and over-working the clay.

A look at each error individually, with suggestions for corrections, will help one to avoid these errors.

1. Throwing with improperly wedged clay.

Success on the wheel can only be achieved with a thoroughly homogeneous clay, free of air bubbles. In an effort to eliminate trapped air, incorrect wedging may amplify the problem, instead of solving it.

The least complicated wedging method is achieved by combining two halves of clay, which have already been cut in half by a tightly stretched wire. When the two halves are joined,

The posibility of entrapping air is eliminated during the wedging process, if contact is first made with the pointed edge of the lower half of clay.

however, it is possible to trap air between them, and form new bubbles.

There is a simple solution to this problem. After cutting the clay in two, slap one half down so that the cut surface is facing away from the potter and is set at a forty-five degree angle. The mass of clay presents a pointed upper edge. As the other half of clay is slapped down onto it, contact is made first at the point, eliminating the possibility of entrapping air. Ten or twelve pounds of clay can be handled comfortably, and cutting the clay thirty or forty times should produce a thoroughly workable mass.

If an occasional air bubble is found in the early stages of throwing, it may be punctured with a needle tool, and compressed as work progresses. If however, an irregularity can still be felt, it is advisable to start anew with another ball of clay.

A potter's view of a correctly centered mound of clay. As the wheel rotates, no eccentric movement should be perceptible in the clay.

This uneven lip is the result of drawing up an imperfectly centered mound of clay.

2. Proceeding with the throwing process before the clay is truly centered.

Trying to throw with clay that is not truly centered produces cylinders that wobble, have uneven tops, and vary in wall thickness. Only a very experienced potter can cope with these problems.

Proper centering calls for skillful use of the hands and arms. Correct balance and support from the large muscles of the body aid greatly in the control of the clay. True centering is only achieved when no lateral movement is discernible. As the wheel spins, the clay should look and feel as if it is motionless.

3. Misjudging bottom thickness.

This error results in a pot that is either bottom heavy or bottomless. Confidence and skill in judging bottom thickness are quickly acquired with the use of a simple aid—a needle tool. Mark the needle three-eighths of an inch from the point, using a strip of masking tape. As the opening process on the wheel nears completion, the wheel is stopped and the tool is inserted into the clay floor, until the needle touches the wheel head. The impression made by the wider section of the needle, covered by tape, indicates how much deeper the opening should go. As skill and technique are acquired a standard and uniform thickness of one-fourth inch is usually used for most pots under twelve inches. For very small or large pots the thickness is adjusted proportionately. The three-eight inch wall thickness used in this learning step is simply easier for the beginning potter to manipulate.

Soon the ability to judge bottom thickness by sight and feel alone is learned. Any holes made by the needle are closed in subsequent throwing. Guesswork is eliminated. Bottom thickness is no longer a problem.

4. Inability to thin the lower portion of the cylinder wall.

A pot may be trimmed, and walls made thinner when hard as leather, but proper throwing techniques require the ability to shape

19

cylinders with walls as thin at the bottom as at the top. Most cylinders thrown by beginners have walls which are excessively thick in the lower half. The solution to this problem is found in the correct use of the left hand, first when widening the opening, and then when drawing up the walls. The left hand must provide the dominant pressure from within the cylinder. A small ring of clay should ride up the cylinder and precede the hands as they draw up the walls. Clay must move from the bottom of the cylinder to the top. This movement allows the form to grow taller.

Judging lower wall thickness, visually, is very deceptive. Here too, the taped needle tool may be used to give an indication of thickness. Insert the needle into the wall from the outside, stopping when the point begins to emerge from the inner wall. The enlarged hole made by the tape indicates excessive thickness.

Needle checking in this manner still leaves the cylinder in a workable state. Cutting the cylinder in half with a wire will expose the wall thickness when practicing, but the cylinder must be discarded.

5. Inability to keep the cylinder walls parallel.

Centrifugal force works against us in the upper section of the growing cylinder. The thinning walls tend to flare out, producing a cylinder narrow at the base, wide at the top. The controlling action must come from outside the cylinder. At the start of the drawing up stage, we have seen how the left hand must exert the dominant pressure to keep the lower wall thin. As the hands ride up to one-half the height of the cylinder, pressure is equally exerted. Past this point, the right hand assumes the main thrust to counteract the centrifugal pull. This containing action maintains the cylindrical shape.

6. Over-wetting and over-working the clay.

Clay will continuously absorb any free water present. Unfortunately, this absorption causes the strength of the clay to deteriorate. The separation between minute clay particles is

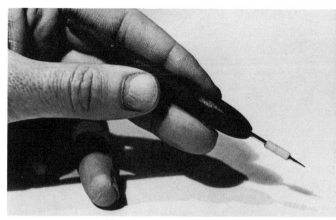
The needle tool can be adapted for checking thickness of the walls.

The needle tool can also be used to test bottom thickness.

increased as more water seeps between them, thus destroying the natural cohesiveness of the material.

Limiting the working time and rationing the amount of water added in the drawing up stage will ensure a workable clay throughout the entire throwing process. When the walls are thin, the clay is most vulnerable to excessive absorption of water. For the final stages of throwing, the clay should be as dry as possible. If wetting is necessary, slip—watery clay—should be used instead of water.

Acquiring the skills of throwing will not be quick and easy, nor will success be instantaneous. All of the frustrations of learning to throw will not disappear. However, an ability to solve these six common potter's problems will aid greatly in achieving success on the wheel.

The flared out upper wall of this cylinder is due to an inability to counteract the centrifugal force.

The corrective measure to realign the flared wall is shown here, both hands collaring in the form.

Lower wall thickness is tested.

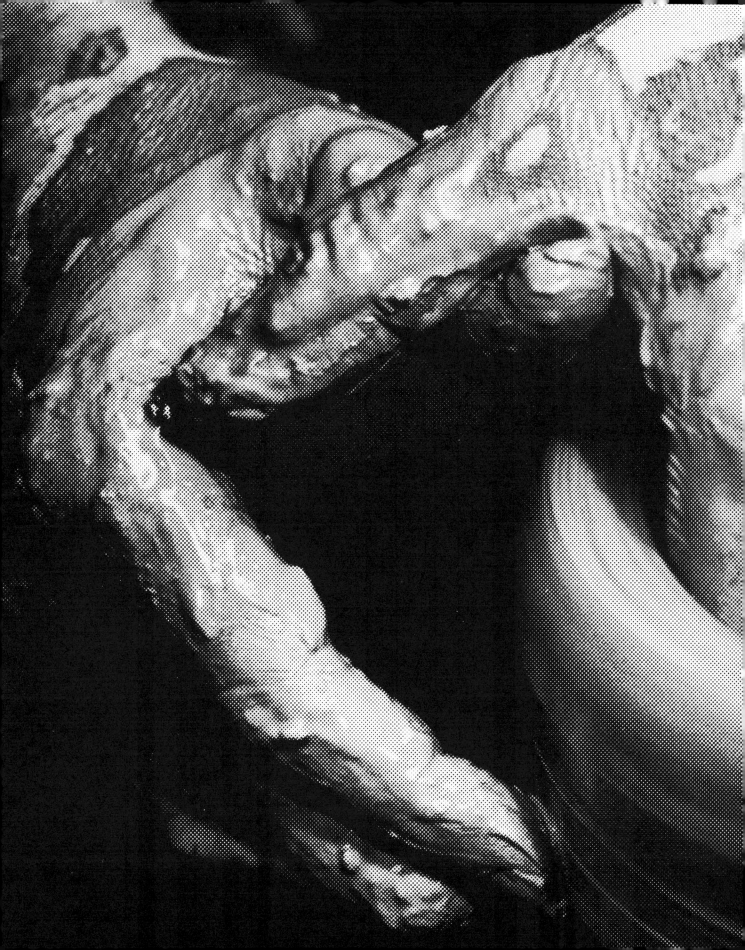

4
Throw a Cylinder

Throw a Cylinder

The cylinder serves as a vehicle for learning the basic throwing skills. Once achieved, it may be transformed into a mug, a canister, a lamp, a trumpet, an elegant vase or other objects of one's own invention. These items all belong within the realm of the cylinder.

The goal of this initial step is to shape a clay cylinder that has thin walls and an even thickness from bottom to top. Acquiring this ability to control, shape, and produce a symmetrical object from a spinning, chaotic, cohesive mound of earth will be a positive first step in a series of learning experiences that can be frustrating, rewarding, demanding, and magical. The technical skill acquired here will be summoned again and again, and will form the foundation for all wheel throwing.

The eventual height that this basic cylinder will attain is dependent upon the amount and cohesiveness of the clay as well as the ability of the potter. A ball of well-wedged clay is first slapped onto the central portion of the wheel head. The clay must be maneuvered into a symmetrical mound, in the exact center of the spinning disc, before any further manipulations take place. Centering is facilitated by a fast wheel speed (at least one hundred rpm), the application of water as a lubricant, and muscular coordination and control.

Once true centering is achieved, one may begin the opening. To establish this central depression, the thumbs, riding atop the solid clay mound, gradually press downward. A fast wheel speed is maintained. If friction develops, the addition of water will eliminate the resistance. As the depth increases, a needle tool, as previously mentioned, may be used to probe and test the remaining thickness.

Next, the opening should be widened, particularly at the bottom. This step will not only establish the cylinder floor, but will facilitate the

The throwing of a cylinder begins with the centering of a ball of clay.

Both thumbs press downward into the rotating mound to open the clay.

24

The opening is widened and the cylinder floor is established. The fingers of the left hand, inside the cylinder, move the clay into the palm of the right hand, riding outside the cylinder.

The first draw up of the cylinder wall. The wheel is slowed for all subsequent steps.

The final draw up. The cylinder is brought to full height.

next act of drawing up the cylinder wall. Beginners have difficulty preventing walls from becoming excessively thick in the lower portion. Widening the opening will also aid them in drawing up walls that are uniformly thin.

The first drawing up of the cylinder wall requires firm compaction of the clay. The knuckle of the right hand index finger presses against the outer surface, the tips of the first two fingers of the left hand press from within, riding the clay wall in a gradual, continuous upward motion. A ring of clay should ride up the cylinder, just above the fingers.

Following this first draw up of the wall, the wheel speed should be slowed to approximately 60 rpm. For the remaining throwing processes, the tip of the right hand index finger is used instead of the knuckle. Finesse is more important than strength.

When the goal of throwing thin walled, symmetrical cylinders is achieved, this cylinder may be utilized, with a minimum of alteration, to produce an endless variety of finished pieces subject to individual invention. Among these may be the following items:

Mug

Because correlation exists between the amount of clay used, the height of the cylinder, and the degree of difficulty, a mug is an ideal beginners project. A one pound ball of clay is used to throw a small cylinder, approximately four and one-fourth inches high, and three and one-half inches wide. Attachment of a handle turns the learning cylinder into a functional mug. The handle may either be "pulled," cut from a slab, or pressed into a mold.

Vase

Striking effects are achieved when a tall cylinder is utilized as a vase. As a means of preserving all the height achieved in the cylinder, a separately thrown top section is added.

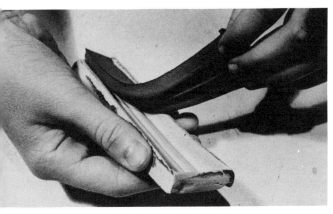

A handle may by formed by pressing clay into a bisque mold or by pulling it.

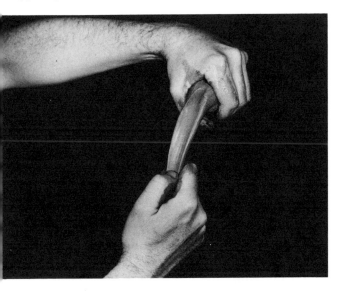

An embossed clay stamp is used to press the handle on to the leather hard mug.

A cluster of mugs.

Vase, created from two pieces using the basic cylinder for the bottom section. Forming the upper lip section on the wheel.

Joining the lip section to the basic cylinder. Both sections are semi-dry.

A wooden tool is used to fuse the seam. These tool marks are left as a decorative element.

Canister

To produce a canister, the cylinder is used, unaltered except for a slight groove formed in the upper lip to form a seat for the lid. This cover may be formed as a flat disc on the wheel, or cut from a slab of clay. Handles may also be attached.

Cone(Vase/Trumpet)

Constriction of the walls will transform a cylinder into a conical shape. Pressure from both hands against the exterior surface will cause the cylinder to narrow and grow taller. An additional consequence of this collaring action is a thickening of the walls. To counteract this thickening, the walls are again thinned with the left hand inside the cone and the right hand exerting the dominant thrust from the outside.

The inverted cone that results from the constriction of the cylinder wall can form a vase or any other item that one can invent. For example, the many years of my youth, spent practicing and performing on the trumpet, have left an indelible mark on my thinking process. This led to an inevitable experiment. I threw a bottomless vase, fired it, and played a tune on it.

Lamp

The combination of a clay cylinder and a light bulb can produce a handsome lamp. Expansion of the clay cylinder's upper wall is accomplished by an outward thrust, supplied by the index finger of the left hand, from within the cylinder

A variety of items into which the basic cylinder may evolve.

The fingers of the right hand serve to control this outward expansion.

A disc of clay is added inside the cylinder, joined when both components reach a semi-dry state. This disc will serve as a mounting platform for the socket. Attachment of the electric cord, the on-off switch, the socket and the bulb to the glazed cylinder will complete the project.

The several items that have been presented, all conceived within the cylindrical form are intended to stimulate the creative thought process of the student potter. Functional, non-functional, and abstract objects may proliferate. Acquired skill will allow invention and innovation.

A basic cylinder, fitted with cover and handles, makes a useful canister.

Pressure from the index finger of the left hand within the cylinder, expands the lip in preparation for forming a seat for the lid. A wooden palette is used to control this expansion.

A chisel-faced wooden tool forms a well-defined seat for the cover.

To throw the lid, a small ball of clay is first centered into a flat disc with an excess of clay left in the center. This excess is then opened, drawn up, and a knob is formed.

With the wheel stopped, a pair of calipers are used to check the size of the lid. A lid with a diameter measurement one-eighth of an inch smaller than the canister opening will assure a proper fit when dried and fired.

Alteration of the cylinder is accomplished by pressure from both hands, collaring in the cylindrical form, transforming it into an inverted cone.

Completed stoneware vase.

A ceramic trumpet.

Once the cone narrows to a degree that makes the inside inaccessible, a sponge stick is substituted for the left hand.

The basic cylinder, thrown bottomless, expanded at the top, fitted with clay disc, a socket, and a globe bulb, functions as a lamp.

A cross section of the lamp, showing the clay mounting disc, socket, socket mounting, globe bulb, wire, and on-off switch.

The index finger of the left hand exerts a gentle pressure from within, causing the upper wall to expand. The fingers of the right hand control this expansion.

5
Throw
an Oval

A variety of items that may evolve from the oval form.

Throw an Oval

The next step in the potter's wheel learning process will be aimed at acquiring the skills needed to alter the cylindrical form into an oval. An outward pressure, originating from within the cylinder, will cause the walls to bulge. In addition to this pressure, shaping may be accomplished by the position of the two hands in relation to one another. When the hands are not directly opposite one another on either side of the wall, a change of wall direction will occur. When the inside hand rides above the outside hand an outward thrust takes place. When the outside hand is the one that rides above, an inward thrust results. Learning to execute and control this shaping process will be the present goal. When manual control and dexterity are gained, a multitude of new design concepts become possible.

Difficulties that are usually encountered in first attempts at shaping the oval include a loss of symmetry, excessive wall thinning, and total collapse. If the wall is extended gradually, symmetry is maintained. To avoid excessive thinning of the expanding wall, during the preliminary drawing up stage an extra thickness should remain at the mid-point of the intended bulge. Avoiding over-extending, over-working, and over-wetting the clay will help to prevent total collapse.

When throwing ovals that will have very narrow openings, it is advantageous to maintain a narrow top throughout the entire throwing process, because once the bulge is formed, extensive contraction of the upper section is difficult. As an aid to throwing bulging shapes with narrow necks, a small sponge, tied or glued to the end of a dowel, is used to reach through the narrow opening and to exert an outward thrust. The sponge serves as a substitute for the left hand. To contain and control this outward thrust, a rubber kidney tool may be used in the

The final draw up.

Before the wall is expanded, the top is narrowed.

This sponge tool will provide the outward thrust from within.

right hand, outside the oval form, just opposite the sponge.

The functional vases illustrated here are just two of the infinite possibilities into which the oval form may evolve.

Oval Vase

In the vase illustrated, the oval form is narrowed at the top, and a flared lip is formed, resulting in a graceful unified entity.

Variations as to the degree of swelling, and the location of its apex, lend different attitudes to pots. Also, the degree of difficulty in maintaining symmetry during the throwing process is compounded by the degree of swelling.

Square Vase

As an additional alternative, which can also serve as a masking device to hide a lack of symmetry in early attempts, the oval may be squared when semi-dry. The change from a round to a square pot is a gradual one, accomplished through several transformations. By pressing a side of the pot down against a flat surface, a plane is established. The second side to be altered should be opposite the first. The remaining two sides are flattened in a similar manner. The process is repeated several times, until the adjoining flat planes meet, and corners are formed.

The expansion of the wall alters the cylinder into an oval. The right hand rides outside, opposite the sponge, to contain and control this expansion.

The opening is narrowed.

An oval vase with a narrow lip.

Narrowing the opening in the basic oval, in preparation for forming the lip.

Forming the lip, as the wheel slowly turns.

A variety of vases, all based on the oval.

44

Four semi-dry vases, prior to alteration.

The same four vases, after squaring.

Alteration of a vase.

6
Throw
a Bowl

Throw a Bowl

The function of the cylinder as a prerequisite form, when shaping objects on the potter's wheel, has been demonstrated. However, bowl throwing is an exception to this procedure, as the bowl form does not evolve from the cylinder, and requires several different techniques.

The centering and opening processes are identical to those used in throwing cylinders. However, once the centered mound is opened, the technique changes. To form a foundation for a bowl, the heel of the left hand is used to maneuver the clay wall in an outward direction. This movement of clay is peculiar to bowl throwing.

A low, flat-bottomed bowl—even though its configuration is similar to that of a low cylinder—is classified with bowl throwing, since, in the forming stage, it is necessary to transport a mass of clay across the wheel head.

As a compensation for the speed gained by working at the outer edge of the wheel head, the wheel should be slowed to approximately 40 rpm when shaping and thinning the bowl walls. This thinning is accomplished with the hands in the traditional posture, index finger of the left hand compressing the inside surface, right hand index finger compressing the outside surface. Thumbs should establish contact with each other, when possible, to coordinate the action of both hands.

The degree of outward thrust, and the amount of overhang that the bowl wall will withstand, again is determined by the cohesiveness of the clay and by the degree of moisture content.

When throwing round-bottomed bowls, the hands move in an outward and upward direction. This diagnoal movement adds to the complexity of the thinning process. When extending the walls, one should avoid deep finger indentions, as these grooves weaken the wall and contribute to the possibility of collapse. Use of a kidney tool aids in maintaining a smooth surface and helps preserve symmetry.

It is advisable, when shaping the rim, to slightly thicken the leading edge. This added thickness not only serves as a protection against chipping, but also provides a surface to hold the glaze, as glaze, made fluid by the heat of the kiln, tends to run off the sharp edges. The thickened lip also contributes an aesthetic element, balancing and ending the visual upward thrust of the wall.

The techniques of bowl throwing will be demonstrated in the following presentations.

Round-bottom Bowl

The traditional bowl shape, similar to bowls thrown by the ancient Chinese potters, is an appropriate starting project. The dimensions of the finished bowl should be consistent with the ability of the student potter.

The technique of cutting a foot or base into the leather hard bowl is also demonstrated. This method of forming a foot, first perfected centuries ago in China, is aimed at providing the bowl with a positive setting in the kiln. The foot acts as a deterrent to warpage, and creates a slight but graceful lift in the appearance of the bowl.

Footed Bowl

The combination of two forms, opposite in shape and manner of throwing, results in an elegant and graceful bowl. A separately thrown cylindrical foot is added to the bowl when both components are semi-dry and trimmed. Varying the height of the foot, and the shape of the bowl provides an endless variety of design possibilities.

Clock

A clock is one possible use of a bowl in a totally unorthodox way. Here, a flat-bottomed bowl is thrown. It's eventual function will be to house a battery operated clock movement. A separately thrown base section completes the

A variety of bowl forms.

form, imparting the look of modern sculpture to the ceramic work.

With the acquisition of bowl throwing skills, the basic techniques of forming ceramic objects on the potter's wheel are learned. An opportunity to review, perfect, and expand these skills follows.

The basic bowl—an oval.

This step is unique to bowl throwing. The palm of the left hand moves the clay outward.

Thinning the bowl wall.

A rubber kidney tool is used to refine the bowl interior.

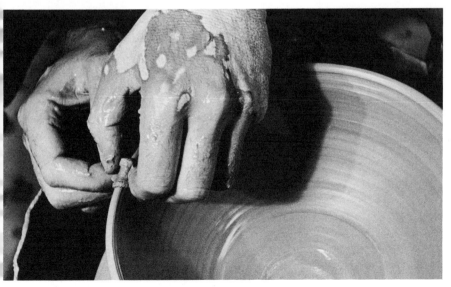

A chamois is used to smooth the edge of the wall.

The leather hard bowl is inverted in the center of the wheel head, and secured with small wads of clay.

A wire cutting tool is used to establish the outer surface of the foot.

Next, the inside of the foot is cut.

A final touch, a plaster stamp signs the bowl.

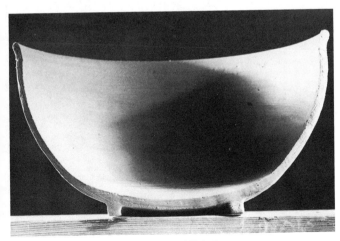

A cross section, showing the foot and wall thickness.

Completed bowl with a cut foot.

The two components of this footed bowl, in the leather hard state.

To assure a symmetrical bowl, a line is scribed into the bottom of the slowly rotating bowl.
This line indicates where the foot will be set.

Fusing the seam.

The flat-bottom bowl and the cylinder that will form the clock.

A stoneware clock, using a flat-bottom bowl to house the mechanism.

The base cylinder is altered.

Fusing the seam with a wooden tool.

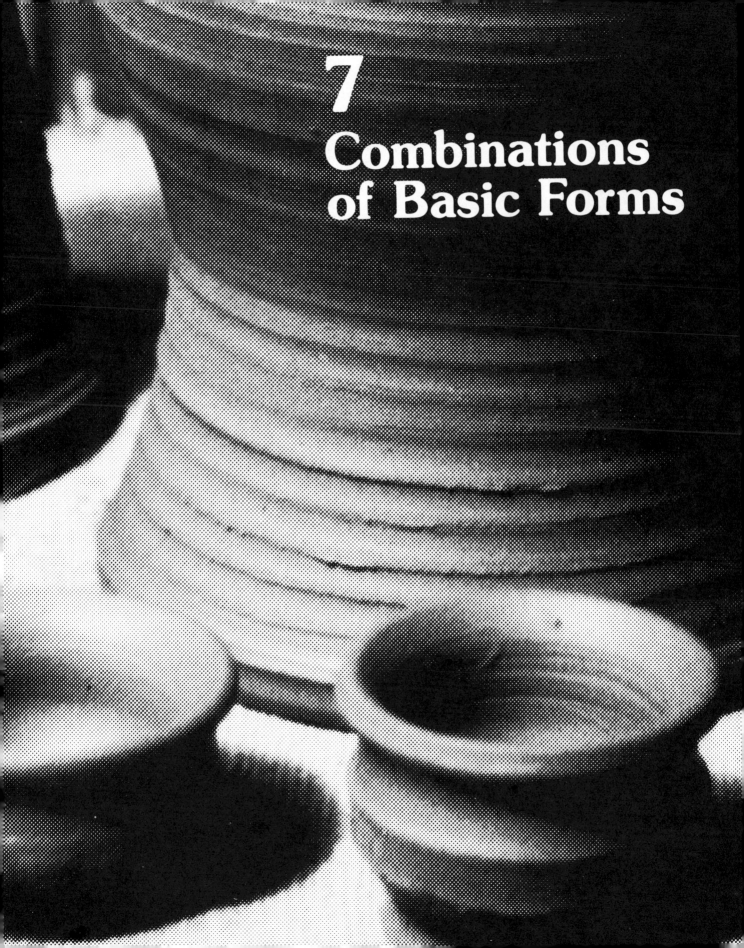

7
Combinations
of Basic Forms

Combinations of Basic Forms

If we may paraphrase Cezanne, all products of the potter's wheel are derived from the cylinder, the cone, the oval, and the bowl. To provide an opportunity for reviewing and refining these basic shapes, products combining these various forms will be made.

When joining leather hard clay components, all surfaces that meet should be scored with a needle tool, and painted with slip, just prior to fusion. This application assures a crack-free seam. It is also advisable, when drying combined clay forms, that the rate of drying be extremely slow. For the first twenty-four hours following completion, the work should be kept under a plastic cover to allow the various moisture levels of the components to equalize.

There is an endless variety of objects that can be made from a combination of basic forms. The throwing and construction of two possible products—a candelabrum and an oil lamp—will be demonstrated here.

Candelabrum

Seven components are united to form a holder for three candles. The center form is cylindrical in its lower half and is oval shaped above. The arms are cone shaped, and the setters for holding the candles are miniature bowls.

An additional challenge is present: multiple throwing of duplicate forms. Two identical cones, and three identical candle holders are required.

Oil lamp

The original predecessor of this oil lamp materialized in the early Greek civilization of 700 B.C. In this modern version, the attachment of two cones to an oval results in a functional oil lamp.

The technique of foot cutting is used again. Since the lip of the oval form does not have the structural strength to support the upended pot, a chuck is used to cradle it during trimming. A similar chuck may be made by first throwing a thick ring of clay. After a bisque fire, the ring is glued to a bat or disc.

Cooking oil or lamp oil will serve as a contemporary substitute for olive oil. Fill half the bowl and insert the wick, feeding it first through the spout. Capillary action will keep the absorbent wick supplied with oil, the small pores in the wick drawing up the oil much as a blotter lifts ink. The lamp illustrated burns for approximately three hours.

Two functional ceramic products, constructed by a combination of the basic shapes are shown. The challenge remains for the student to invent and create individual combinations. Personal preference may now dictate final objectives. Whether the finished object is functional, non-functional, realistic or abstract, the decision rests with the student.

The seven components that are joined to construct the candelabrum.

The neck section is joined to the base.

Painting on slip prior to joining the arm sections. Notice the hole cut into the base. This hole allows free circulation of air throughout all the sections.

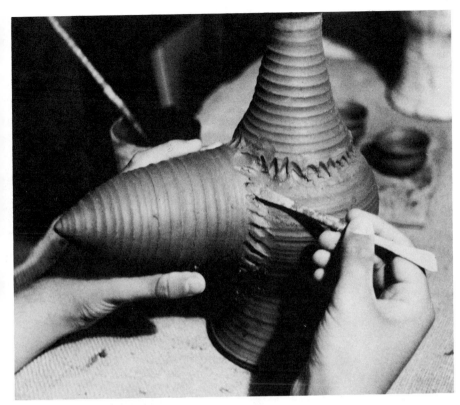

Joining the arm section to the base.

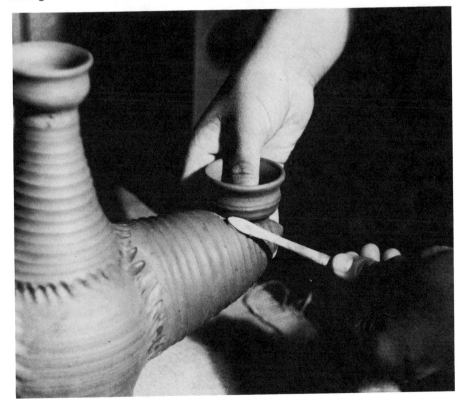

The candle holder is attached.

Forming the wick spout.

Forming the lamp's handle on the wheel.

The three components that will be combined to form the oil lamp.

A chuck is used to cradle the inverted oval form during foot-cutting.

The handle is pressed on.

After exit holes are cut for the wick, the spout is pressed on.

63

8
Double Wall
Cylinder
Throwing

Double Wall Cylinder Throwing

The unique has a magnetism, an appeal to the learning mind that the ordinary just does not have. For the student who possesses the basic ability to throw the previously presented forms, and who now is looking for "new worlds to conquer," throwing double wall cylinders is ideal. As the name suggests, an unusual cylinder will be formed on the wheel, differing from previous forms. Here, two cylinders are drawn up from the centered mound, one inside the other.

Several possible ceramic pieces using this unique cylinder, a planter with a built in drainage dish, a bird feeder, and a ring-vase, are demonstrated.

Planter

Using clay to hold earth and a growing plant seems only appropriate. Originally, the earth and its atmosphere, with the passage of time, transformed feldspathic rock into clay. Earth, plant, clay, and glaze are thus all compatible.

The outer wall of the double cylinder is shaped to form a drainage dish. A slight variation in the design results in a hanging planter. The lip should be turned out, and three equidistant hanging holes cut when semi-dry. The finished planter, suspended by leather thongs, is ideal for indoor or outdoor gardening.

To avoid eventual rotting of the leather thongs, be certain the hanging holes are set above the soil level. An alternate choice could be, when working in the leather hard stage, to add loops of clay to the external wall for thong attachment.

Bird Feeder

The double wall cylinder is fitted with a cover to create a bird feeder. The center cylinder

For double wall cylinders, the goal of centering is a low flat mound.

A sponge is pressed into the rotating mound, forming a moatlike depression. The placement of this depression designates the amount of clay the inner and outer wall will have.

serves as a reservoir for storing the bird seed, and the outer wall is shaped to form the feeding trough. Holes cut into the reservoir allow the trough to be automatically replenished with bird seed. The cover, in addition to protecting the reservoir, has a brim that extends over the feeding platform, protecting both the feed and the birds from the elements.

Leather thongs are used to suspend the feeder. Knots tied in the appropriate places also hold the lid up, which allows for easy refilling.

Ring-Vase

To produce this unusual vase, the double wall cylinder is thrown with an open center. The resulting donut shape is then uprighted, and a separately thrown base and lip are added.

The ring form is adaptable to many design considerations. Mirror or picture frames are possibilities. The rings may be stacked, cut, and combined in endless variations. Ceramic utensils, sculptures, or even pieces of furniture are other possibilities. The only restriction is the necessity of an exit hole to allow for the escape of air. All other limits are set only by the kiln size and our imagination.

With the fingers of both hands riding in the moat, the central section is opened. A bottom may be left or the opening may proceed through to the wheel head, depending on the item to be thrown.

The opening in the central section is widened.

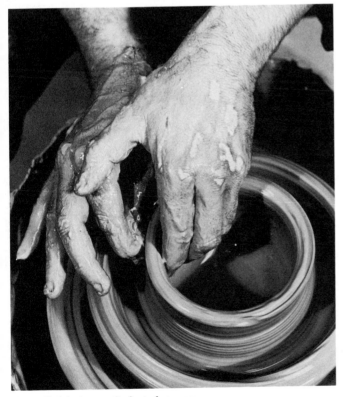

The wall of the inner cylinder is drawn up.

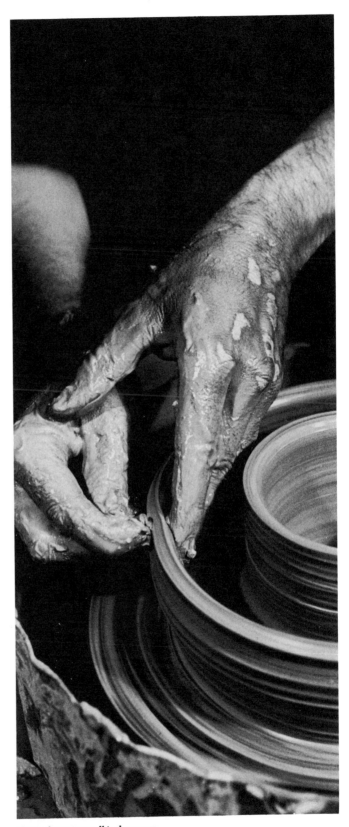

Next, the outer wall is drawn up.

When throwing the double cylinder for the planter, more clay is left in the central section. This extra amount allows the inner cylinder wall to be drawn up higher. Here, the outer wall is being shaped.

The planter, on the wheel, at the end of the throwing session.

The drainage holes are formed by pushing a pointed plastic rod through the semi-dry clay wall. Three equidistant holes prove sufficient for excess water run off.

When shaping the inner cylinder, a real challenge exists in extending it over the drainage dish.

A semi-dry planter set behind two completed, glazed planters.

Drawing up the inner wall. As in the planter, the central section requires more clay so that it can be drawn higher than the outer cylinder.

The completed bird feeder.

The final draw up of the central cylinder.

A chamois is used to smooth the upper lip.

The outer cylinder wall is shaped.

Forming the lid, on the wheel. It is thrown in an inverted position.

A pointed plastic rod is used to form the suspension holes.

A needle tool is used to cut holes for automatic replenishment of the bird seed.

A cross section, showing both cylinders, and the holes.

For the ring-vase, the center opening is pressed down to the wheel head, and both walls are extended to equal height. Here, the inner wall is flared out.

Next, the outer wall is curved in.

The walls are brought into proximity, then they meet.

The entrapped air lends a buoyancy to the clay form. It is cut from the wheel head with a wire, and inverted.

A wire tool is used to trim the bottom.

Grooves are pressed into the clay, making both sides similar.

These three components form the ring vase.

The base section is fused.

A hole is cut into the top, slip is applied, and the lip is set in place.

The upper seam is fused, completing the ring-vase.

9
Sculpture from Wheel Thrown Forms

The basic oval, closed at the top, at the completion of the throwing process.

Sculpting begins with the addition of embossed clay slabs to delineate the eyes.

The surface is developed further, with wooden tool marks to simulate feathers.

The addition of small clay pellets adds textural interest.

Sculpture from Wheel Thrown Forms

In this chapter we will explore another facet of the wheel's capabilities—using it as an aid in creating sculpture.

Clay has a number of qualities that allow it to be shaped, squeezed, bent, extruded, embossed, and incised. It is not only cohesive, but is the most manageable, pliable sculptural medium available. It is sensitive enough to reproduce a fingerprint, and once fired, permanent enough to enable that fingerprint to survive for thousands of years.

Even with these attributes, ceramic sculpture has not found favor with contemporary sculptors. For the sculpture to survive the glaze or final fire that gives it permanence, the sculpted form must be hollow with uniformly thin walls. These restrictions are easily met by the potter's wheel.

Animals

A menagerie of animals may be constructed from the oval wheel thrown form. Parrots, buffalo, hippopotami, anteaters, creatures from sea and land, imagined or real, may spring from the potter's wheel.

The owl is used to demonstrate a beginning sculpture, since the alterations to its thrown form are minimal. After a symmetrical oval form has been thrown on the wheel, it should dry in normal conditions (room temperature 68° on a dry day) for about six hours. At this stage of the drying process, the form is firm enough to maintain its shape when handled, yet pliable enough to be altered without creating crack-lines in its surface. The oval form can now be sculpted or can be covered with plastic to keep it in this workable state.

A thick slip is stippled on to further enhance the surface.

The completed owl, ready for drying and firing.

An abstract ceramic sculpture, derived from the oval and cylinder forms.

The two components, dried to a leather hard state, are ready to be sculpted.

A wire is used to cut out a portion of the oval.

A ten percent (10%) addition of fine or medium grog, added during the wedging process to any throwing body, will make the clay suitable for sculpture. The grog makes the clay more porous, helping to reduce shrinkage and warpage, also providing an escape route for gases during the firing stage.

Abstract Sculpture

In this demonstration, a wheel thrown, closed oval is modeled to form an abstract sculpture. After drying to a leather hard state, a wire is used to cut out a section, producing a negative area within the oval. To contain and delineate this negative area, a slab of clay is added. The base is opened to provide free circulation of air.

Other possibilities within the abstract realm include a combination of ovals and a use of segmented ovals.

Heads

Modeling the human form in clay has fascinated artists throughout history. Clay heads stare at us from antiquity, their anonymous creators leaving tangible evidence of man's inner drive to create in the image of himself. Whether sculpting to fulfill a spiritual need, as the ancient Chinese who populated their tombs with life-sized ceramic figures, or to fulfill an artistic need, each civilization has left terra cotta works for future generations to study and enjoy.

This project is rich in possibilities. One can sculpt an imaginary or idealized head, fictional character, a person of historical importance, king, a clown, or a family member. A rudimentary knowledge of the anatomical structure of the face and skull combined with accurate observation, will assist in the creation of any kind of head. Armed with this knowledge, caricatures and abstract variations may also be attempted.

Two thrown forms, a head shaped oval and a neck shaped cylinder, can serve as the skeletal structure. Manipulation of the clay is facilitated

The cut-out section is removed.

Prior to joining, the area that forms the seam is scored and slip is painted on.

The seam is fused.

To further delineate the negative area, a slab of clay is added.

The slab is trimmed.

A metal kidney tool is used to refine the surface.

Heads sculpted from wheel thrown forms.

by having access to the interior of the sculpture. A hole cut in the top allows a hand to be placed inside. The hands, working together, expand and compress the clay wall.

As work progresses, rotation of the sculpture, allowing observation of all contours, helps greatly in establishing the desired proportions. Observation from above and below will also provide a visual confirmation of correct modeling.

Another aid in checking the modeling is the use of a portable light. By moving the light while observing the shadow line, the artist can determine how the sculpture will appear in various angles of light.

The closed oval clay form that will become the head.

The oval is set on the neck shaped cylinder.

A needle tool is used to cut an access hole into the top of the head.

The hand inside breaks through the oval, and the seam is fused. This opening of the oval will allow air free circulation throughout the sculpture.

The clay wall is manipulated to form eye sockets.

Clay is added to form the nose.

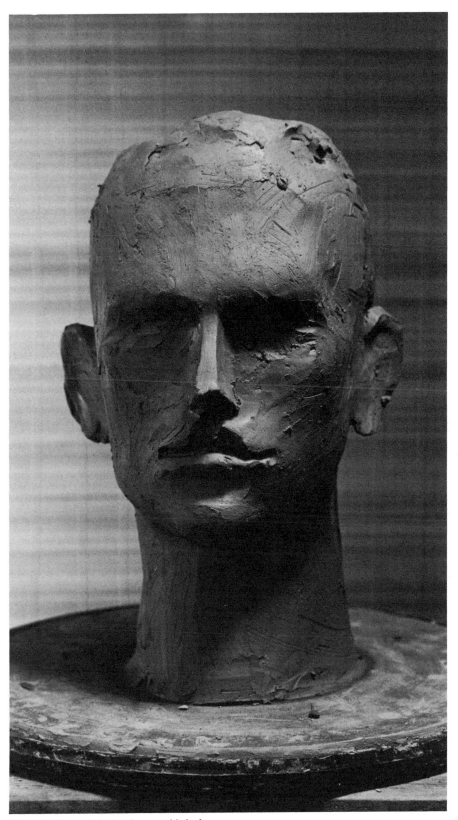

The basic planes of the head are established.

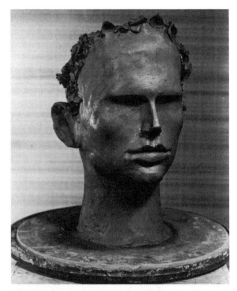

The hair line is established, and the surface refined.

In the modeling of the hat, a clay stamp is used to emboss the surface.

Modeling of the ears completes the sculpture.

"John", a life size stoneware sculpture, also sculpted from thrown forms.